This book belongs to

_____

This book is dedicated to my children - Mikey, Kobe, and Jojo.

Copyright © 2023 Grow Grit Press LLC. All rights reserved. No part of this book may be reproduced in any form without permission in writing from the publisher. Please send bulk order requests to info@ninjalifehacks.tv

Paperback ISBN: 978-1-63731-802-7
Hardcover ISBN: 978-1-63731-804-1
eBook ISBN: 978-1-63731-803-4

Printed and bound in the USA.
NinjaLifeHacks.tv

Ninja Life Hacks®
by Mary Nhin

I could tell you my body in measurements -
I know exactly my **arm**'s length!

From my **finger** tip to my **elbow**
And all the way up my arm,

I know the power of my upper body
Which helps me do no harm.

My **hands** are my strongest weapons,
Each one is full of might.
I channel all my energy through them,
When I'm in a ninja fight!

I flatten my hand and chop,
As I proudly yell "KI-AI!"
My hand can cut through wood or boards,
As long as I start real high.

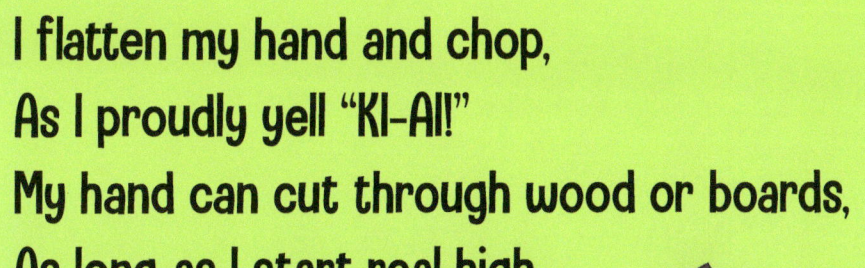

/kiːˈaɪ/ pronounced "KEY" "I"

My **hips** help me flex and pivot,
As I slide under fences and beams.

A ninja must be nimble,
And I'm more flexible than I seem.

My **thighs** are full of leg muscle,
Which I use any time I squat.
It may seem like that's not often,
But I actually do it a lot...

When I'm ducking from a sword,
Or when I'm crouching to get down low,
Sometimes I'll do a squat walk,
When I quietly have somewhere to go.

My **knees** help me with kicking,
They bend and give me force.

When I am feeling extra flexible,
I can tackle any obstacle course.

My **feet**, just like my hands,
Help me activate my might.
But first they help me creep quietly
In the darkness of the night.

I can walk or hop or run with them
To get where I need to be.
When I need to, I can kick with them.
When I need to go fast, they help me flee.

Some of my strongest body parts
Are the ones above my neck.
They hold my special ninja skills,
And keep the rest of my body in check.

My **eyes** help me as a ninja
By helping me see things far away.
My vision is great at nighttime,
But it's even better during the day.

My **ears** help me hear the quietest noises, I like to listen carefully.

TICK TOCK

They help me find my missions,
And complete tasks successfully.

My **nose** picks up the scents
When I point it to the air and sniff.

Sometimes I can find my target
Just by taking in a big whiff.

My **mouth** helps me make a whistle
When I need a distraction.

Of all of my body parts,
There is one that brings me the most pride.

Without my smarts and intuition,
What kind of ninja would I be?
My **heart** is my favorite body part
Because it's what makes me me!

www.ingramcontent.com/pod-product-compliance
Lightning Source LLC
Chambersburg PA
CBHW041523070526
44585CB00002B/61